Daily Readings with
St Isaac of Syria

The Daily Readings Series
General Editor: Robert Llewelyn

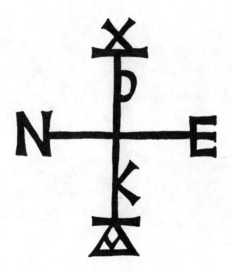

Daily Readings
with
St Isaac of Syria

Introduced and edited by
A. M. Allchin

Translated by Sebastian Brock

Templegate Publishers
Springfield, Illinois

First Published in 1989 by
Darton, Longman and Todd Ltd
89 Lillie Road, London SW6 1UD

Introduction and arrangement
© 1989 A. M. Allchin
Translation © 1989 Sebastian Brock

ISBN 0-87243-173-8

First published in the United States in 1990 by
Templegate Publishers
302 E. Adams St./P.O. Box 5152
Springfield, Illinois 62705

Contents

Introduction

THE MAN IN HIS TIME

St Isaac the Syrian, or St Isaac of Nineveh, as he is also known, is one of the greatest spiritual writers of the Christian East. If one visits the monasteries of Mount Athos or Romania today and asks the monks whom they would recommend for spiritual reading, the name of Isaac will nearly always be among the first to be mentioned. His influence on Orthodox spirituality continues to be great. It is by no means confined to the monasteries. Traces of it can be seen in the works of one of the greatest Russian novelists, Fyodor Dostoevsky.

Isaac himself, however, was a member of a Church from farther East than the world which we usually call Eastern Orthodox. He was born in the province of Qatar, on the western shore of the Persian Gulf, some time in the first half of the seventh century. His references to ships and sailors make us suspect that he may have lived near the sea. In the 660s he became for a short time Bishop of Nineveh, in what is now Northern Iraq. After only five months he retired from public life as a bishop, and returned to the silence of the monastic way. This is the background from which his writings come.

The Church to which he belonged, the Church of Persia, or the Church of the East, was one of those Churches outside the Byzantine Empire which had their own independent existence, and in the course of time came to be suspected of heresy. Historians often speak of this Church as Nestorian. Whether or not the accusation is true is another matter. What is certain is that this was a Church of immense missionary activity. In Isaac's own century it succeeded for a time in establishing flourishing Christian communities as far east as China, and across much of Central Asia.

From our point of view, however, it is more important to notice that this was a Church which used Syriac as its principal language. Syriac is a language very closely allied to Aramaic, the language which Jesus spoke. This, therefore, was a Church with a Semitic culture and a Semitic outlook. We shall see that Isaac quotes the Gospels with great freedom and to great effect.

It was also a Church with a very rich tradition of prayer and spirituality, which had constantly had to face persecution and repression. One of the first and certainly one of the greatest of all Christian hymn-writers, St Ephraim the Syrian, comes from this tradition. Isaac is a worthy representative of a later phase of its development.

It is noteworthy that in his writings Isaac never speaks about the controversies over the person and nature of Christ, the disputes which led to the divisions between Chalcedonians, Monophysites and Nestorians. In fact his words about the dangers of passionate arguments over doctrine (60 and 61) suggest that he may have purposely avoided speaking of these subjects.

What is clear is that the Church to which he belonged was in his century becoming more and more isolated from the Churches farther West — Constantinople, Antioch and Rome — on account of the Arab invasions and the spread of Islam. It was being forced into following its own way.

All this is not altogether irrelevant to us. For Christians who live at a time when the Churches are still divided, and are sometimes torn apart by controversy and debate, it is good to hear the voice of one who, in a different age of controversy and division, managed to go beyond such differences and speak words of wisdom whose authority was recognized in all three main sections of the Eastern Christian world.

Reading St Isaac we cannot doubt for a moment that he was intensely concerned for the truth of the Gospel and the truth of the faith. But through his life of prayer he had learned to live it and express it in ways which, through the centuries, have crossed all kinds of frontiers, linguistic and cultural, as well as ecclesiastical and political. The multitude of translations of his work into Greek and Georgian, into Arabic and Amharic, into Russian and Romanian, bears witness to the continuing vitality of his teaching in Eastern Christendom.

THE MAN AND HIS MESSAGE

But is it possible that his work will be able to speak across the chasms which divide East from West, the seventh from the twentieth century?

11

It will be for the reader to decide.

For myself I can only say that there are words here which once heard are never forgotten, words which speak with the clarity and vigour which we find in the Gospels themselves: 'Like a handful of dust thrown into the sea are the sins of all mankind compared with the mercy and providence of God' (63). 'Blessed is he who has eaten of the bread of love, which is Jesus' (25).

Who, having read Isaac's account of the compassionate heart, 'a heart on fire with love for all creation' (29), is ever likely to forget it? When we come to his description of how the animals are attracted to the man in whom humility reigns, we are reminded of St Francis (69). But then we remember that St Francis was not the only saint with whom the animals made friends. Such stories abound in the history of Christian sanctity, from St Columba on sixth-century Iona to St Seraphim in the forests of nineteenth-century Russia. They tell us of the restoration of our true humanity.

But Isaac can also tell us much about the inner journey of the human spirit. Within each one of us the Kingdom is to be found, the Kingdom whose sun is the light of the Holy Trinity, whose air is the very breath of the life-giving Spirit (52). There are mysteries of silence and of stillness here, in which the heart of the man of prayer makes silent melody, speaking 'in a hidden way to the hidden God' (53). It is not by chance that his writings have been so much treasured among the hesychasts of Eastern Orthodoxy. The word hesychast is one which applies to the man or woman of prayer who seeks to live a life of silence and stillness, who feels called into the desert places of the heart.

What kind of man was Isaac? He was clearly a monk who wrote in the first place for his fellow-monks. Some of them were men who were living as hermits in great physical solitude. More often, it seems, they were living in their own little houses, near enough to one another to have contact with their brethren. Indeed, they were near enough at all times to be aware of a conflict between the call of charity and the call to prayer.

Isaac gives us a vivid picture (38, 39) of a man whose life of prayer was intense indeed, but who none the less was ready to give shelter to an ailing brother. He was also one who was not above giving a hand with plastering and decorating when there were cells to be built up or repaired. Isaac is very insistent that, for the one who has received it, the call to prayer has an absolute priority. When God speaks, man must obey. But he is also quite clear that 'an ascetic without compassion is a tree that bears no fruit' (81). The two commandments of love are so inseparably intertwined that they cannot be divided.

He makes it very evident that the solitary life can only be lived, in a Christian context, on the basis of a strong faith in, and experience of, the solidarity of us all, both in Adam and in Christ, both in suffering and in glory. Time and again he reminds us that we are members one of another, that our life is with our brother. It is very striking to see which of the Desert Father stories he chooses to retell (28). There is nothing private or privatized about such a way of life, however solitary it may be. All are present in the prayer of each.

Isaac can be, like the Gospels, exceedingly severe and exceedingly gentle. He is certainly not without a sense of humour. We can see it in his recommendations about how to deal with talkative visitors, a method which goes back to the time of the Desert Fathers (71). We can see it too in his gruff comment about 'the way of ease'. 'We know where the easy way leads!' (30). There is something here of the humour with which Father Kelly of Kelham would end a retreat address with the words: 'And then you might miss being crucified, and that would be a pity.'

There can be no doubt whatsoever in these pages about the absolute demands which the Gospel makes on those who hear it. The religion which Isaac describes is fervent and total in its claim. It transforms man both inwardly and outwardly. There is no separation here between body and soul. Both are intimately concerned. That is why we hear so much about fasting, so much about tears and prostrations.

Through the experience of the cross, through dying to this world, we find already here and now the joy of the resurrection, made present in our world of space and time. That is a joy which looses all bonds, which gives us a first taste of the world to come.

Ultimately, Isaac's vision is one of the whole creation restored in Christ. The animals are part of it, including the reptiles. Remember that he lived in a desert and would have met real snakes. Even, and this is more mysterious, the demons are not altogether left out. The man in whom God's love is at work will pray also for them.

We face here a very different attitude to heaven and hell from that which for many centuries has been dominant in the Christian West, whether Catholic or Protestant. Heaven and hell are not two parallel and comparable realities, equally stable, equally unalterable. Isaac tells us that we do not know when the end of hell will be, and in doing so, at least hints that hell can have an end (82). We may, indeed we must, pray and hope for all. We are reminded of the story of the Russian monk of our own time, Staretz Syluan, who, when someone spoke about the eternal punishments of atheists, simply said: 'Love could not bear that. We must pray for all.'

We touch here on very mysterious realities. In his own century Isaac seems at times to have been criticized for teaching openly things that many people thought were better kept secret. His teaching that in God mercy has wholly conquered justice could be a case in point (57, 58). Undoubtedly the hope and prayer that in the end 'all shall be well and all manner of thing shall be well' has been more firmly planted at the heart of Eastern Christianity than it has been in the West. With us it is only recently that the optimism of grace which we find in Julian of Norwich has begun to outbalance the pessimism of judgement which for centuries has weighed so heavily on the Western Christian mind.

Isaac needs to be read as a whole. The reality of damnation as an inner possibility for each one is often with him. Like some of the great Western mystics, he sees that the fire of hell must be the fire of God's love (83). He does not underestimate the tragedy of sin. But he is overwhelmed by his sense of God's grace in bringing us into existence in the first place. Still more he is amazed that after sin and after death that grace should raise us up into newness of life. In the face of this love there can be no place for despair (59). If man's sin is great, God's love is always greater.

THE PRESENT SELECTION

Isaac wrote a great deal: almost 400 large pages in the recent American edition. It would be possible to make many different selections from him which would give very different impressions of his teaching. He says different things in different places and does not seem to worry if at times he seems to contradict himself.

While I have tried to represent something of the variety of his teaching, I have purposely chosen passages which, it seems to me, speak directly to our twentieth-century situation. They all come from a monastic setting but they are not exclusively monastic in concern.

I have left aside most of the detailed instructions about fasting and vigil and the mastery of the passions. Somewhat reluctantly I have quoted only a little of what he says about the further stages of the life of prayer. There are difficult problems here about the correct translation and interpretation of some of the Syriac terms, which could scarcely be dealt with in a book such as this.

However, something of the quality of this teaching on prayer can be gathered even in so small a compass: his wisdom and moderation about terminology (45); his conviction that there comes a moment in prayer when prayer ceases and we are taken beyond prayer (42); his description of prayer in the Spirit (53); his insistence that much in this area can only be understood on the basis of direct experience (41).

I have, however, quoted a number of passages which have a bearing on his understanding of humility (64-70). For him humility is much more than a moral quality. It is the essential characteristic of God himself as he wills to become incarnate for the salvation of the world. God himself is infinitely humble in his dealings with creation. When his creatures themselves become humble, then they become truly like him. They become as it were transparent. All his glory shines through them, and all things come together in peace around them.

MORE TO COME

We have not yet said the most surprising thing

17

about the text of St Isaac's works, and that is that there is more to come. In the summer of 1983, Dr Sebastian Brock found in the Bodleian Library in Oxford a Syriac manuscript containing the second part of Isaac's work which was long thought to have been lost. What we have now is only about half of the whole. So we have almost as much again of the writings of this superlative spiritual teacher, as a kind of divine gift to encouarge us in the difficulties which beset us in our century. All who read this book should pray for Dr Brock and his collaborators that they may find the time and energy for the long and complex work of editing and translating this text.

There have so far been two editions of St Isaac's work in English. The older was made by the Dutch scholar, A. J. Wensinck, and is translated directly from the Syriac: *Mystic Treatises by Isaac of Nineveh,* 1923. The more recent, *The Ascetical Homilies of St Isaac the Syrian,* was produced by the Holy Transfiguration Monastery, Boston, Massachusetts in 1984. The translation was made by Mr Dana Miller, who also provides a long and informative introduction and epilogue.

Passages from St Isaac are also to be found in Sebastian Brock's recently published anthology, *The Syriac Fathers on Prayer and the Spiritual Life* (Cistercian Publications/Mowbrays, 1987). This book is indispensable for anyone who wants to know more about the spiritual tradition from which St Isaac comes. I am deeply indebted to Dr Brock for making the translations which are used in the present book, and for his constant help and encouragement.

A. M. ALLCHIN

18

Boldness in prayer

Sit in the presence of the Lord every moment of your life, as you think of him and recollect him in your heart.

Otherwise, when you only see him after a period of time, you will lack freedom of converse with him, out of shame; for great freedom of converse is born out of constant association with him.

Constant association with fellow-beings involves the body, whereas when it is with God, it involves the soul's meditation and the offering of prayers.

As a result of its great intensity, this meditation is sometimes mingled with wonder: 'The heart of those who seek the Lord shall rejoice.'

Seek the Lord, O sinners, and be strengthened in your thoughts with hope.

Seek his face through repentance at all times – and you shall be sanctified by the holiness of his face. You shall be purged clean of your wickedness.

Run to the Lord, all who are wicked; he forgives wickedness and removes sins.

The vision of faith

Faith is the gateway to mysteries. What the eyes of the body are to sensory objects the same is faith to the eyes of the mind as they gaze on hidden treasures.

We have two eyes of the soul, just as we have the body's two eyes, as the Fathers say.

But these do not both have the same function of sight: with one we see the hidden glory of God which is concealed within nature, together with his might, his wisdom and his eternal thought for us, all of which can be perceived through his special providence for us.

With the same eye we also behold the spiritual orders, our fellow-beings.

But with the other eye we behold the glory of God's holy nature.

When our Lord wishes to admit us to spiritual mysteries, he opens wide the sea of faith in our minds.

The gift of repentance

Repentance has been given to humankind as a grace beyond grace. Repentance is a second birth from God, of which we have received an earnest in baptism; we receive it as a gift by means of repentance.

Repentance is the gateway to mercy which is open for all who seek it. By way of this gate we enter into the divine mercy, and apart from this entrance one cannot find mercy.

For 'all have sinned', according to divine Scripture, 'and are justified freely by grace'.[1] Repentance is the second grace and is born in the heart as a result of faith and fear.

Fear is the paternal rod which guides us as far as the spiritual Eden; but once we have reached there it leaves us and turns back.

Eden consists in divine love, wherein is the paradise of all blessedness. This is where St Paul received supernatural sustenance.

After having tasted of the tree of life, he exclaimed, saying, 'Eye has not seen, nor ear heard, nor has it entered the human heart, what God has prepared for those who love him'.[2]

1. Rm 3:23–24.
2. 1 Co 2:9.

The blessing of humility

Be despised and rejected in your own eyes, and you will see the glory of God within yourself. For where humility blossoms, there God's glory bursts forth.

If you strive to be slighted openly by all men, God will magnify your honour. If you are humble in your heart, then in your heart he will show you his glory.

Learn how to be despised, while being filled with the Lord's honour, rather than how to be honoured, while you are smitten within.

Blessed is he who has humbled himself in all things, for he will be exalted in all. For someone who for God's sake humbles himself and thinks meanly of himself, is glorified by God.

The person who hungers and thirsts for God's sake, God will make drunk with his good things, with the wine whose inebriation never leaves those who drink it.

He who goes naked for God's sake is clad by him in raiment of glory. He who becomes poor and in need for God's sake, is strengthened in consolation by his true riches.

Despise yourself for God's sake, and without your being aware of it your glory will become great.

The feast of the Kingdom

The tree of life is the love of God from which Adam fell away. Thereafter he met with joy no longer, but toiled and wearied himself in the land of thorns.

Until we find love, our labour is in that land of thorns: amidst thorns we both sow and reap, even if our seed is the seed of righteousness. We are pricked all the time, and however much we render ourselves righteous, we live by the sweat of our brow.

But once we have found love, we partake of the heavenly bread, being nourished without labour and fatigue.

The person who has found love eats Christ at all times, and from then on he becomes immortal. Whoever eats this bread, he says,[1] shall never taste death.

Blessed is the person who has eaten of the bread of love, which is Jesus.

Whoever is sustained on love is sustained by Christ who is God over all. Jesus testifies to this, saying, 'God is love'.[2] This is the air in which the righteous find delight at the resurrection.

Love is the Kingdom in which the Lord mystically promised that his disciples should eat and drink.

1. Jn 6:58.
2. Jn 4:16.

Love from God

Love which stems from created things is like a small lamp whose light is sustained by being fed with olive-oil.

Again, it is like a river fed by rainfall; once the supply that feeds it fails, the surge of its flow abates.

But love whose cause is God is like a spring welling up from the depths: its flow never abates, for God alone is that spring of love whose supply never fails.

Love of the brethren

Love the poor, that through them you may find mercy.

Do not go near quarrelsome people, otherwise you will be forced to abandon your habitual peaceful state.

Do not feel disgust at the loathsomeness of different illnesses, for you too are clothed in flesh.

Do not make things worse for those that are bitter at heart, lest you be scourged by the same rod that they are; then you will seek someone to console you, but will find no one.

Do not reject those who are deformed from birth: will you not enter Sheol along with them?

Love sinners, but reject their works. Do not despise them for their faults, lest you be tempted by the same ones.

Remember that you share in the stink of Adam and that you too are clothed in his infirmity.

Perfect love

Abba Agathon, who was more experienced than all the solitaries of his time, was a man who loved and honoured stillness and silence more than anyone else.

He once went to a festival in order to sell his handiwork; there he found a stranger lying sick in the street, so he rented a house and stayed with him, working with his own hands, spending what he earned on the man and on paying the rent of the house. He served the sick man thus for six months, until he recovered.

It is said that Abba Agathon used to say, 'I should like to find a leper, give him my body and take his in exchange.' Here we have perfect love.

The compassionate heart

An elder was once asked, 'What is a compassionate heart?' He replied:

'It is a heart on fire for the whole of creation, for humanity, for the birds, for the animals, for demons and for all that exists. At the recollection and at the sight of them such a person's eyes overflow with tears owing to the vehemence of the compassion which grips his heart; as a result of his deep mercy his heart shrinks and cannot bear to hear or look on any injury or the slightest suffering of anything in creation.

'This is why he constantly offers up prayer full of tears, even for the irrational animals and for the enemies of truth, even for those who harm him, so that they may be protected and find mercy.

'He even prays for the reptiles as a result of the great compassion which is poured out beyond measure – after the likeness of God – in his heart.'

By way of the cross

The blessed Apostle openly calls it a gift for someone to be ready in faith for suffering for the sake of his hope in God. Thus he says, 'To you it has been granted by God not only to believe in Christ, but also to suffer for his sake.[1]

As St Peter wrote in his letter, 'When you suffer for righteousness' sake, blessed are you, for you will become sharers in the sufferings of Christ'.[2]

Therefore when you are at ease and enjoyment do not rejoice; and when tribulations come upon you, do not be sullen or consider this as something alien to the way of God.

For this path of God has been trodden from all the ages and through all generations by means of the cross and death.

Where do you get the idea that the afflictions on the path do not belong to the path? Do you not wish to follow in the footsteps of the saints? Do you want to travel by some special path of your own, one that does not involve suffering?

The path to God is a daily cross. No one has ascended to heaven by way of ease. We know where the easy way leads!

1. Ph 1:29.
2. 1 P 3:14; 4:13.

Following Christ

Do not be astonished if, when you begin to practise virtue, severe tribulations break out against you on every side.

Virtue is not accounted virtue if it is not accompanied by difficulty and by labours.

That is why all those who in the fear of the Lord wish to live in Jesus Christ will suffer affliction.

For he says, 'Whoever wants to follow me, let him deny himself and take up his cross and follow me. If anyone wishes to save his life in comfort, he will lose it; if anyone shall lose his life for my sake, he shall find it.'[1]

For this reason, then, our Lord placed before you the cross, that you might sentence yourself to death, and then send forth your soul to go after him.

---

1. Mt 16:24; 10:39.

Desperation

Nothing is so strong as desperation. It knows no defeat at the hand of any, whether on the right hand or the left.

When someone has cut off in his mind all hope of life, no one is more daring than he; no foe can face him, no rumours of affliction can weaken his purpose, for every affliction which may come is less than death, for he has resolved to accept death for himself.

If, in every place and in every circumstance, and on every occasion in all that you intend to do you set your mind's sight on toil and affliction, then you will find yourself at all times courageous and unhesitating in standing up against all apparent difficulties.

Through the power of your deliberation, the timidity that is customarily born in people whose thoughts are set on comforts, will take flight.

Not only this, but all difficult and hard things which you may encounter will appear easy and light for you.

Indeed, it can often happen that your affairs turn out in the opposite way to what you had expected, and these things may not touch you.

God's love for us

The sum of all is that God the Lord of all, out of fervent love for his creation, handed over his own Son to death on the cross. 'For God so loved the world that he gave his only-begotten Son for its sake.'[1]

This was not because he could not have saved us in another way, but so that he might thereby the better indicate to us his surpassing love, so that, by the death of his only-begotten Son, he might bring us close to himself.

Yes, if he had had anything more precious he would have given it to us so that our race might thereby be recovered.

Because of his great love, he did not want to use compulsion on our freedom, although he would have been able to do so; but instead he chose that we should draw near to him freely, by our own mind's love.

1. Jn 3:16.

For the life of the world

Out of love for us and in obedience to his Father, our Lord joyfully took insult and suffering upon himself, as Scripture says, 'For the joy that he possessed he endured the cross, despising the shame'.[1]

For this same reason our Lord said on the night when he was betrayed, 'This is my body which is given for you, for the salvation of the world; and this is my blood which is shed for all, for the remission of sin'.[2]

And, 'For their sakes I sanctify myself'.[3]

It is the same with all the saints: when they become perfected, they attain this accomplishment by imitating God in the outpouring of their love and compassion upon all humanity.

The saints seek for themselves this sign of likeness to God – to be perfected in the love of their neighbour.

1. Heb 12:2.
2. Mt 26:26, 28.
3. Jn 17:19.

A prayer

Hold me worthy, O Lord, to behold your mercy in my soul before I depart from this world; may I be aware in myself at that hour of your comfort, along with those who have gone forth from this world in good hope.

Open my heart, O my God, by your grace and purify me from any association with sin.

Tread out in my heart the path of repentance, my God and my Lord, my hope and my boast, my strong refuge, by whom may my eyes be illumined, and may I have understanding of your truth, Lord.

Hold me worthy, Lord, to taste the joy of the gift of repentance, by which the soul is separated from co-operating with sin and the will of flesh and blood. Hold me worthy, O Lord, to taste this state, wherein lies the gift of pure prayer.

O my Saviour, may I attain to this wondrous transition at which the soul abandons this visible world, and at which new stirrings arise on our entering into the spiritual world and the experience of new perceptions.

Prayer at night

One day I went to the cell of a holy brother, and because of an illness lay down in a corner, so that he could take care of me for the sake of God, for I had no one else to go to in those regions. For some time I had seen this brother's custom of waking at night for the Office before the other brethren, and he would commence going through the psalms, however many they might be, but then, all of a sudden, he would abandon his Office and fall on his face: he would strike his head on the ground sharply in quick succession, some hundred times one might guess – all this stemming from the fervour which had been kindled by grace in his heart. Then he would stand up, greet the cross, again make a prostration, again greet the cross, and again fall on his face.

He acted in this manner a great many times, so that you could not keep count: has anyone the ability to count the prostrations which that brother made each night? He would approach the cross and kiss it some twenty times with fear and ardour, with love mingled with reverence; and then he would continue to recite the psalms again. But every now and then, no longer able to endure the mighty flame of the thoughts which kindled him with their fervour, he would raise his voice, being overcome with joy, unable to contain himself. And I was greatly astonished at the grace to be found with that brother who was so eager and wakeful in the work of God.

Work by day

After the morning Office, when he sat down to read the Bible he became like a man enraptured: with every verse he read he would fall many times on his face, and at many of the phrases he would raise his hands to heaven and glorify God many times over. He was about forty years old, his food was sparse, and in temperament he was dry and warm. Because he used to constrain himself in ways his frame would not accept, he often looked like a shadow.

He was compassionate, and extremely bashful. He showed his compassion joyfully, and his nature was pure; very open to any request, he was wise in God. Because of his luminous joy he was beloved by everyone: he was everyone's favourite. He worked with all the brethren in their cells with the clay whenever this was available. This would be for three or four days at a time, and he would return to his cell only in the evening, continuing thus until the work of the brethren was completed. Moreover, when he worked with the brethren, he did so because of his modesty, and he forced himself to do it, since he did not like to leave his cell – for he spoke to me many times of his aversion to leaving his cell. Such was the divine way of life of that marvellous brother.

Prayer before the cross

At whatever time God should open up your mind from within and you give yourself over to unceasing kneeling, do not give your heart over to care for anything, even though the demons secretly try to persuade you otherwise.

Then look and be amazed at what is born within you as a result.

Do not compare any of the ascetic practices with falling on one's face before the cross night and day, with one's hands clasped behind one's back.

Do you wish that your fervour should never cool and that your tears should never dry up? Then practise this.

Blessed are you if you meditate on what I have told you, and seek for nothing else alongside God night and day.

Your light shall be like the morning's and your righteousness will quickly shine forth; and you will be like a jubilant paradise of flowers and a fountain whose water never fails.

The joy which comes from prayer

Look at what good things occur to someone as a result of divine care!

Sometimes, when a person is on his knees at the time of prayer, with his hands outspread or extended heavenwards, his eyes gazing on the cross, and with the whole movement of his mind, as it were, stretched towards God in entreaty, during the time while such a person is thus engaged in supplications and groanings, all of a sudden a fountain of sweetness is stirred up from his heart.

His limbs become feeble, his sight dim, he bows his head; his thoughts are altered and he can no longer kneel on the ground as a result of the exultation at the sign of grace which surges through his entire body.

Therefore, my reader, pay attention to what you are reading. Indeed, can such things as these be known from writings in ink? Can the taste of honey pass over from a written text to the palate of the reader?

If you do not strive, you will not find; and if you do not knock eagerly at the door and keep long vigil before it, you will not receive an answer.

Beyond prayer

Delight during prayer is different from vision during prayer. The latter is superior to the former, just as a fully grown man is superior to a small child.

Sometimes biblical verses themselves will grow sweet in the mouth, and a simple phrase of prayer is repeated innumerable times, without one having had enough of it and wanting to pass on to another.

And sometimes out of prayer contemplation is born; this cuts prayer off from the lips, and the person who beholds this is like a corpse without soul in wonder. We call this the faculty of 'vision in prayer'; it does not consist in any image or portrayable form, as foolish people say.

This contemplation in prayer also has its degrees and different gifts, but up to this point it is still prayer, for thought has not yet passed into the state where there is non-prayer, for there is something even more excellent than prayer.

For the movements of the tongue and of the heart during prayer act as the keys; what comes after these is the actual entry into the treasury: from this point onward mouth and tongue become still, as do the heart – the treasurer of the thoughts –, the mind – the governor of the senses –, and the bold spirit – that swift bird –, along with all the means and uses they possess. Requests too cease here, for the master of the house has come.

Beyond definitions.

The Fathers have the habit of designating by the word 'prayer' every excellent impulse, and every spiritual capacity. And not just these, but the blessed Interpreter also includes good actions under the heading of prayer, even though it is obvious that prayer is one thing and actions which are carried out are another thing.

But sometimes they designate as 'contemplation' what they elsewhere call 'spiritual prayer'; or sometimes they term it 'knowledge' or 'revelations of spiritual things'.

You see how varied are the terms used by the Fathers in spiritual matters. Precise terms can be established only for earthly matters; for matters concerning the New World this is not possible: all there is is a single straightforward awareness which goes beyond all names, signs, depictions, colours, forms and invented terms.

For this reason, once the soul's awareness has been raised above this circle of the visible world, the Fathers employ whatever designation they like concerning this awareness, since no one knows what the exact names should be.

On silence

Love silence above everything else, for it brings you near to fruit which the tongue is too feeble to expound.

First of all we force ourselves to be silent, but then from out of our silence something else is born that draws us into silence itself.

May God grant you to perceive that which is born of silence! If you begin in this discipline I do not doubt how much light will dawn in you from it.

After a time a certain delight is born in the heart as a result of the practice of this labour, and it forcibly draws the body on to persevere in stillness.

A multitude of tears is born in us by this discipline, at the wondrous vision of certain things which the heart perceives distinctly, sometimes with pain, and sometimes with wonder.

For the heart becomes small and becomes like a tiny babe: as soon as it clings to prayer, tears burst forth.

Thirst for Christ

Thirst for Jesus, so that he may inebriate you with his love.

Blind your eyes to all that is held in honour in the world, so that you may be held worthy to have the peace which comes from God reign in your heart.

Fast from the allurements that make the eyes glitter, in order that you may become worthy of spiritual joy.

Prayer accords strictly with behaviour. For no one yearns for heavenly things when he is bound up in the fetters of the will concerning bodily matters; nor is there anyone who will ask for things divine when he is occupied with earthly matters.

Everyone's desire is made known by his actions, and it is for the things about which he is concerned that a person will be anxious to ask. The person who desires the greatest things is not concerned with the lesser.

Answers to prayer

If God is slow to grant your request and you do not receive what you ask for promptly, do not be grieved, for you are not wiser than God.

When this happens to you, it is either because your way of life does not accord with your request, or because the pathways of your heart are at odds with the intention of your prayer.

Or it may be because your inner state is too childish by comparison with the magnitude of the thing you have asked for.

It is not appropriate that great things should fall easily into our hands, otherwise God's gift will be held in dishonour, because of the ease with which we obtain it.

For anything that is readily obtained is also easily lost, whereas everything which is found with toil is preserved with care.

Acquire freedom within

Honour the labours involved in keeping vigil, so that you may discover consolation close at hand within your soul.

Persevere in reading in stillness, so that you may be drawn towards the wonder of God at all times.

Love poverty with patience, so that your mind may be recollected from wandering.

Detest superfluity, that you may be preserved from confusion of mind.

Withdraw from multitudinous affairs and have your own conduct as your concern, so that your soul may be saved from any fragmentation of its interior tranquillity.

Acquire purity by your conduct, so that your soul may shine with joy during prayer, and that at the remembrance of death joy may be kindled in your mind.

Acquire freedom by your way of life, so as to be freed from turmoil. Do not bind your freedom by what affords you pleasure, lest you become a slave of slaves.

Our weakness and God's help

Blessed is the person who knows his own weakness, because awareness of this becomes for him the foundation and beginning of all that is good and beautiful.

For whenever someone realizes and perceives that he is truly and indeed weak, then he draws in his soul from the diffuseness which dissipates knowledge, and he becomes all the more watchful of his soul.

But no one can perceive his own weakness unless he has been remiss a little, has neglected some small thing, has been surrounded by trials, either in the matter of things which cause the body suffering, or in that of ways in which the soul is subject to the passions. Only then, by comparing his own weakness, will he realize how great is the assistance which comes from God.

When someone is aware that he is in need of divine help, he makes many prayers. And once he has made much supplication, his heart is humbled, for there is no one who is in need and asks who is not humbled. 'A broken and humbled heart, God will not despise.'[1]

As long as the heart is not humbled it cannot cease from wandering; for humility concentrates the heart.

1. Ps 51:17.

The power of prayer

Once a person has become humble, straightaway mercy encircles and embraces him; and once mercy has approached, immediately his heart becomes aware of God helping him, since he discovers a certain powerful assurance stirring within him.

When someone has become aware of the coming of divine help, and that it is this which aids and assists him, then at once his heart is filled with faith, and from this he understands that prayer is: the haven of help, the fountainhead of salvation, a treasury of assurance, a saving anchor in time of storm, an illumination to those in darkness, a staff for the weak, a shelter in time of trials, a source of recovery at the time of sickness, a shield of deliverance in war, an arrow sharpened in face of enemies.

Having found an entry to all these excellent things through prayer, henceforth that person will rejoice in the prayer of faith, his heart exulting in confidence – no longer blindly, or through lip-service only, as had previously been the case. Once aware of this, he has acquired prayer in his soul, like a treasure. Out of the joy he experiences he will change the direction of his prayer, turning it into utterance of thanksgiving. This corresponds to what was said by Evagrius, wise among the saints and ready for every eventuality, namely that 'Prayer is joy which gives rise to thanksgiving'.

The Kingdom within

The spiritual country of the person who is pure in soul is within him.

The sun which shines within him is the light of the Holy Trinity. The air which the inhabitants of that realm breathe is the strengthening and all-Holy Spirit. The holy and bodiless beings make their abode within him.

Christ, the light of the Father's light, is their life, joy and happiness. Such a person is gladdened at every moment by his soul's contemplation, and he is held in wonder at the beauty which lies within him, a beauty which is truly a hundred times more resplendent than the brilliance of the sun itself.

This is Jerusalem and the Kingdom of God, lying hidden within us, as the Lord says.[1] This country is the cloud of God's glory into which only the pure of heart may enter, so as to behold the countenance of their Master, having their minds enlightened by the rays of his light.

1. Lk 17:21.

Prayer in the Spirit

A person is deemed worthy of constant prayer once he has become a dwelling-place of the Spirit.

For unless someone has received the gift of the Comforter, in all certainty he will not be able to accomplish this constant prayer in quiet.

But once the Spirit dwells in someone, as the Apostle says, the Spirit never ceases but prays continuously: then whether he sleeps or wakes, prayer is never absent from that person's soul.

If he eats or drinks, goes to sleep or is active; yes, even if he is sunk in deep sleep, the sweet fragrance of prayer effortlessly breathes in his heart.

Then he is in the possession of prayer that knows no limit. For at all times, even when he is outwardly still, prayer constantly ministers within him secretly.

The silence of the serene is prayer, as one of those clothed in Christ says, for their thoughts are divine stirrings.

The stirring of a pure mind constitutes still utterances, by means of which such people sing in a hidden way to the hidden God.

Cleft in the rock

The cell of a solitary is the cave in the rock where God spoke with Moses, according to what the Fathers say.

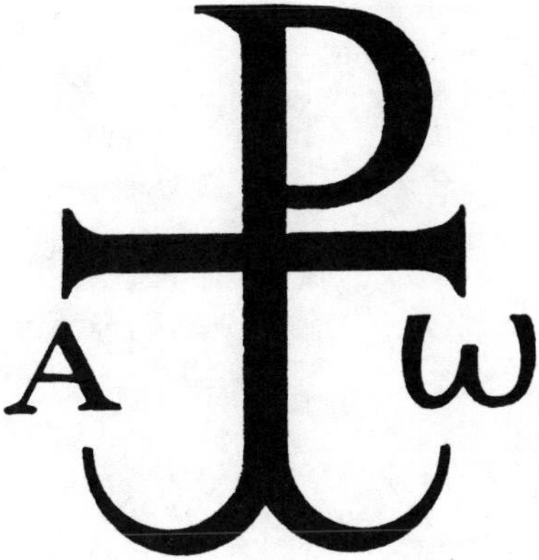

God's goodness

Do not hate the sinner. Become a proclaimer of God's grace, seeing that God provides for you even though you are unworthy.

Although your debt to him is very great, there is no evidence of him exacting any payment from you, whereas in return for the small ways in which you do manifest good intention, he rewards you abundantly. Do not speak of God as 'just', for his justice is not in evidence in his actions towards you.

How can you call God just when you read the gospel lesson concerning the hiring of the workmen in the vineyard? How can someone call God just when he comes across the story of the prodigal son who frittered away all his belongings in riotous living – yet merely in response to his contrition his father ran and fell on his neck, and gave him authority over all his possessions?

In these passages it is not someone else speaking about God; had that been the case, we might have had doubts about God's goodness. No, it is God's own Son who testifies about him in this way.

Where then is this 'justice' in God, seeing that, although we were sinners, Christ died for us? If he is so compassionate in this, we have faith that he will not change.

God does not change

Far be it from us that we should ever think so wicked a thing as that God could become unmerciful. For God's attributes do not change as those of mortals do.

God does not acquire something he did not have before, nor does he lose or increase in what he has, as created beings do. But what God has from the beginning, he has eternally and without end.

Fear God for his love, and not on account of the reputation for sternness which has been attributed to him. Love him, since it is our duty to love him – not for what he will give in the future, but also for what we have already received. Even if it were just this one world which he had created for our sakes, who would be capable of thanking him?

O the wonderful mercy of God! O astonishment at the goodness of God our Creator! O power for which all is possible! O the immeasurable kindness towards our nature which brings even sinners once again to regeneration! Who is sufficient to tell his praises?

Where is the Gehenna that can cause us suffering? What torment is there, the fear of which can prevail in us and overcome the joy of his love? What is Gehenna compared to the grace of the resurrection, when he will raise us from death, causing our corruptible nature to be clad in incorruption, and raising up in glory what was lying in disgrace in Sheol?

The greatness of God's grace

Let all who have discernment come and be filled with wonder. Who has a mind sufficiently wise in order to wonder? Come, let us stand amazed at the grace of our Creator.

The reward of sinners is this: instead of a just reward, God grants them resurrection, and in place of the bodies which trampled on his laws, he robes them in the glory of perfection.

The grace which raises us into new life after we have sinned is greater than the grace which brought us into being when as yet we were not.

Glory to your immeasurable grace! The flood of your grace silences me and no movement is left in me, even to give due thanks.

What lips can confess you, O Good King, who love our life? Glory be to you in the two worlds which you have created, one for our growth, and one for our delight, leading us by all things which you have made to the knowledge of your glory, now and to eternal ages. Amen.

Against zeal

A zealous person never achieves peace of mind. And he who is deprived of peace is deprived of joy.

If, as is said, peace of mind is perfect health, and zeal is opposed to peace, then a person stirred by zeal is ill with a grievous sickness.

While you presume to stir up your zeal against the sickness of others, you will have banished health from your own soul. You should rather concern yourself with your own healing. But if you wish to heal those that are sick, know that the sick have greater need of loving care than of rebukes.

Zeal is not reckoned among mankind as a form of wisdom; rather it is one of the sicknesses of the soul, arising from narrow-mindedness and deep ignorance.

The beginning of divine wisdom is the serenity acquired from generosity of soul and forbearance with human infirmities.

For he says, 'You who are strong should bear the infirmities of the weak',[1] and 'Put right the transgressor with a humble spirit'.[2] The Apostle numbers peace and long-suffering among the fruits of the Holy Spirit.

1. Rm 15:1.
2. Ga 6:1.

Have peace in your heart

Someone who has actually tasted truth is not contentious for truth.

Someone who is considered among men to be zealous for truth has not yet learnt what truth is really like: once he has truly learnt it, he will cease from zealousness on its behalf.

The gift of God and of knowledge of him is not a cause for turmoil and clamour; rather this gift is entirely filled with a peace in which the Spirit, love and humility reside.

The following is a sign of the coming of the Spirit: the person whom the Spirit has overshadowed is made perfect in these very virtues.

God is reality. The person whose mind has become aware of God does not even possess a tongue with which to speak, but God resides in his heart in great serenity. He experiences no stirring of zeal or argumentativeness, nor is he stirred by anger. He cannot even be aroused concerning the faith.

Do not despair

Do not fall into despair because of your stumblings.

I do not mean that you should not feel pain because of them, but that you should not consider them incurable.

For it is better to be wounded than to be dead.

There is indeed a healer: he who on the cross asked for mercy on those who were crucifying him, who pardoned murderers as he hung on the cross.

Christ came on behalf of sinners, to heal the broken-hearted and to bind up their wounds.

The Spirit of the Lord is upon me, he says; for that reason he has anointed me in order to proclaim good tidings to the poor. 'He has sent me to heal the broken-hearted, to proclaim deliverance to the captive, recovery of sight to the blind,'[1] and to strengthen the bruised by forgiveness.

And the Apostle says in his Letter, 'Jesus Christ came into the world to save sinners.'[2] And his Lord also testifies, 'I am not come to call the righteous, for they who are in good health have no need of a doctor; only those who are sick.'[3]

1. Lk 4:18.
2. 1 Tm 1:15.
3. Mk 2:17.

The mercy of God

As a handful of sand thrown into the ocean, so are the sins of all flesh as compared with the mind of God.

Just as a strongly flowing fountain is not blocked up by a handful of earth, so the compassion of the Creator is not overcome by the wickedness of his creatures.

Someone who bears a grudge while he prays is like a person who sows in the sea and expects to reap a harvest.

As the flame of a fire cannot be prevented from ascending upwards, so the prayers of the compassionate cannot be held back from ascending to heaven.

Fear and joy

There is a humility which comes out of the fear of God, and there is a humility which comes from the fervent love of God. One person is humble out of his fear, whereas another is humble out of his joy.

The person who is humble out of fear is possessed of modesty in his members, a right ordering of his senses, and a heart that is contrite at all times.

But the person who is humble out of joy is possessed of great exuberance and an open and irrepressible heart.

Love knows no bashfulness: for this reason she does not know how to give orderly propriety to her members. Love is by nature unabashed and forgetful of moderation. Blessed is the person who has found you, O love, the haven of all joys!

The assembly of the humble is loved of God just as the assembly of the seraphim.

A chaste body is more precious before God than a pure offering. These two, humility and chastity, prepare a tabernacle in the soul for the Holy Trinity.

Humility and peace

No one has understanding if he is not humble, and he who lacks humility is devoid of understanding.

No one is humble if he is not at peace, and he who is not at peace is not humble. And no one is at peace without rejoicing.

In all the paths on which people journey in this world they will find no peace until they draw near to the hope which is in God.

The heart finds no peace from toil and from stumbling-blocks until it is brought close to hope – which makes it peaceful and pours joy into it.

This is what the venerable and holy lips of our Lord said: 'Come unto me all who are weary and heavy laden, and I will give you rest.'[1]

Draw near, he says, to hope in me; desist from the many ways and you will find rest from labour and fear.

1. Mt 11:28.

The clothing of the Godhead

When I wish to open my mouth and to speak on the exalted theme of humility, I am filled with dread, like someone who is aware that he is about to discourse with his own imperfect words concerning God.

For humility is the robe of the Godhead. The Word who became human clothed himself with humility, and thus spoke with us in our human body.

Everyone who has truly been clothed in humility becomes like him who came down from his exalted place and hid the splendour of his majesty, concealing his glory in lowliness, so that the created world should not be utterly consumed at the sight of him.

Creation could not behold him unless he took part of it to himself and thus conversed with it: only thus was creation able to hear the words of his mouth face to face.

The humble man

No one ever hates, or wounds with words, or despises the person who is humble; and because his Lord loves him he is dear to all. Everyone loves him, everyone cherishes him, and wherever he approaches, people look on him as an angel of light and accord honour to him.

A wise and learned man may speak, but they silence him in order to give the humble an opportunity to speak: the eyes of everyone are fixed on his lips, to see what utterance will issue forth from him. Everyone waits on his words as if they were words from God.

The humble man approaches wild animals, and the moment they catch sight of him their ferocity is tamed. They come up and cling to him as to their Master, wagging their tails and licking his hands and feet. They scent as coming from him the same fragrance that came from Adam before the transgression, the time when they were gathered together before him and he gave them names in Paradise. This scent was taken away from us, but Christ has renewed it and given it back to us at his coming. It is this which has sweetened the fragrance of humanity.

Even the demons with their malice and fierceness, with all the pride of their minds, become like dust once they have encountered a humble person.

To acquire humility

Once an elder was asked, 'How can someone acquire humility?' He replied, 'By unceasing remembrance of transgressions, by the expectation of an imminent death, by shabby clothing, by always choosing the last place, by always running to do the tasks that are the most insignificant and disliked, without being forced to; by continual silence, by dislike of gatherings, by desiring to be unknown and of no account, by never possessing as one's own anything at all; by avoiding conversation with all sorts of persons, by disliking profit.

'And after these things, by having one's mind raised above the reproach and accusations of others, and above zealotry; by not being one whose hand is against everyone, and against whom is everyone's hand,[1] but rather one who remains alone and isolated, not taking on the concern of anyone else in the world apart from himself.

'In sum: exile, poverty, and a solitary life, all of which give birth to humility and cleanse the heart.'

---

1. Gn 16:12.

Talkative visitors

Whenever people who love idleness and empty chatter come to you, once they have sat down for a little, then make as though you wish to stand up for the Office. Say, bowing to your guest, 'Brother, stand and let us say the Office, for the time for my Office has already come and I cannot let it pass; otherwise, if I try to perform it at another hour, it becomes a cause of confusion for me. I cannot omit it except for dire necessity, and at present there is no such necessity for me to set aside my prayer.' Do not let him excuse himself from praying with you, and if he says, 'You pray, and I shall be off', then bow to him and say, 'For love's sake, make but one prayer with me, so that I can benefit from your supplication.' Then, when he has consented and you both have stood up, make your Office longer than usual. If you do this each time such people visit you, they will learn that you are not like-minded to them, and that you do not love idleness; accordingly they will no longer come near the place where they hear you are to be found.

From island to island

When a sailor travels across the sea, he watches the stars and by them he steers his ship, using them to direct him to harbour.

But a monk watches prayer because it sets him on the right course, directing him to that harbour towards which his way of life should lead.

A monk gazes at prayer at all times so that it may show him some island where he can moor his ship without fear, and then take on provisions. Then, once again he will set his course to another island.

Such is the voyage of the solitary while he is in this life. He sails from island to island, that is, from knowledge to knowledge, and by his successive change of islands, that is, of states of knowledge, he progresses until he emerges from the sea and his journey terminates at that true city whose inhabitants no longer engage in commerce, but where each rests upon his riches.

Blessed is he whose voyage has not been put off course on this great sea.

Blessed is he whose ship has not broken up, and who has reached harbour with joy.

The pearl of great price

A swimmer dives into the sea naked, in order to find a pearl.

A wise monk journeys through life, stripped of all that he has, to find within himself the pearl, Jesus Christ, and finding him, he no longer seeks to acquire anything else beside him.

Silent praise

From henceforth you will gaze at all times upon the spectacle of God's continual loving care for his handiwork.

Your mind will be swallowed up in awestruck wonder, your senses will be silent, and you, O feeble man, will lie prostrate on your face in prayer, your tongue unable to speak, and your heart incapable of praying; for in wonder at these divine acts even prayer becomes inactive.

This is the inactivity which is superior to work, when a person is completely still in his senses and thoughts, and he lies continually prostrate before his Lord.

Even his bones in their silence will offer up praise to God during this apparent inactivity, as the prophet says, 'All my bones shall say, O Lord, who is like you?'[1]

By this gift, so they say, a person is deemed worthy of the love of God and of perfect humility.

1. Ps 34:10.

The Scriptures

Do not approach the words of the mysteries contained in the Scriptures without prayer and without asking for God's help. Say, 'Lord, grant that I may receive an awareness of the power that is within them.'

Consider prayer to be the key to the understanding of truth in Scripture.

Scripture, the fountainhead

You should understand that the consolation which a solitary receives from external sources – through the movement of the tongue, or by sight or hearing – is inferior to the consolation which stems solely from the heart, without any mediator; this may occur either by means of prayer which is more interiorized than any prayer of the lips, or it may occur suddenly in the mind, manifesting itself without any actual vehicle. Such a revelation belongs to the Spirit, and is a kind of prophecy, for the heart is in fact prophesying, in that the Spirit is revealing to it hidden matters, over which not even the Holy Scriptures have authority; what Scripture was not permitted to reveal, the pure mind is authorized to know – something that goes beyond what was entrusted to Scripture! Nevertheless the fountainhead for all these things is the reading of Scripture: from it comes the mind's beauty.

All these things are born out of the reading of Scripture: even pure prayer itself is born from such reading. Likewise recollection of the mind comes from this reading. Out of it all these things are fashioned.

Good wandering

When you are in prayer, do not ask to be entirely free of mental wandering, which is impossible, but seek to wander following something that is good. For even pure prayer consists in a wandering which follows something – but this wandering is excellent, seeing that the search for something good is excellent. Wandering is bad when someone is distracted by empty thoughts or by pondering on something bad, and so he thinks evil thoughts when he is praying to God.

Wandering is good when the mind wanders on God during the entire extent of his prayer, on God's glory and majesty, stemming from a recollection of the Scriptures, from an understanding of the divine utterances and holy words of the Spirit. For we do not consider as alien to purity of prayer and detrimental to recollection of thoughts in prayer any profitable recollection that may spring up from the Writings of the Spirit, resulting in insights and spiritual understanding of the divine world during the time of prayer. For someone to examine and think in a recollected manner about the object of his supplication and the request of his prayer is an excellent kind of prayer, provided it is consonant with the intention of the Lord's commandment. This kind of recollection of the mind is very good.

Giving

If you give something to someone who is in need then let a cheerful face precede your gift, along with kind words and encouragement for his suffering.

When you do this, the pleasure he feels in his mind at your gift will be greater than the needs of his body.

A person who, while having God in mind, honours everyone, will find everyone to be his helper, thanks to the hidden will of God.

Someone who speaks in defence of a person who suffers injustice will find an advocate in his Creator.

Whoever gives a hand to help his neighbour is helped by God's own hand.

But the person who accuses his brother for his evil deeds will find God as his accuser.

Sayings

The prayer of someone who harbours a grudge is a seed upon a stone.

An ascetic without compassion is a tree that bears no fruit.

A rebuke springing from envy is a poisoned arrow.

The praise of a crafty man is a hidden snare.

A foolish counsellor is a blind watchman: a wise counsellor is a wall of confidence.

Live with vultures rather than with the covetous: live amidst lions rather than among the proud.

Be persecuted, rather than be a persecutor.
Be crucified, rather than be a crucifier.
Be treated unjustly, rather than treat anyone unjustly.
Be oppressed, rather than be an oppressor.
Be gentle, rather than zealous.
Lay hold of goodness, rather than justice.

Sin, hell and death

Sin, Gehenna and death do not exist at all with God, since they are effects, not substances.

Sin is the fruit of self-will. There was a time when sin did not exist, and there will be a time when it will not exist.

Gehenna is the fruit of sin. At some point in time it had a beginning, but its end is not known.

Death, however, is a dispensation of the Creator's wisdom. It will rule only a certain time over nature; then it will certainly disappear.

The scourge of love

The scourges that result from love – that is, the scourges of those who have become aware that they have sinned against love – are harder and more bitter than the torments which result from fear.

The pain which gnaws the heart as the result of sinning against love is sharper than all other torments that there are.

The power of love works in two ways: it torments those who have sinned, just as happens among friends here on earth; but to those who have observed its duties, love gives delight.

So it is in Gehenna: the contrition that comes from love is the harsh torment; but in the case of the sons of heaven, delight in this love inebriates their souls.

God's providence

As soon as someone has come to be raised above the passions, this holy power will attach itself to the soul, not departing from it, either by night or by day, and it will show God's providence to the soul.

And even the minutiae of all that is and that happens, of Yes and No, of what takes place for someone secretly and openly, and of matters relating to the creation of this world – all these are revealed to the soul by the power attached to it, revealing to it God's creative power, and showing it the divine care which unceasingly follows and visits everything which belongs to this created world.

And it shows the soul how this divine care follows a person at all times, and preserves him against adversities at all times, even though he may not perceive this or be aware of it; how it directs him towards what serves for the salvation and the repose of his soul and body, leading to the discovery of his own true life.

Tasting the wellspring

From stillness a person can gain possession of the three causes of tears: love of God, awestruck wonder at his mysteries, and humility of heart. Without these it is unthinkable that anyone should be accounted worthy to taste of the wellspring of flaming compunction arising from the love of God.

There is no passion so fervent as the love of God. O Lord, deem me worthy to taste of this wellspring!

Therefore, if a person does not have stillness he will not be acquainted with even one of these, though he perform many virtuous deeds.

He cannot know what the love of God is, nor spiritual knowledge, nor can he possess true humility of heart.

He will not know these three virtues, or rather, these three glorious gifts.

The humility of greatness

Now humility of heart comes about in a person for two causes: either from precise knowledge of his sins, or from recollection of the greatness of God.

I mean, how exceedingly the greatness of the Lord of all lowered itself, so that in such ways as these he might converse with and admonish men.

He humbled himself so far as to assume a human body, he endured men and associated with them, and showed himself so despised in the world, he who possesses ineffable glory above with God the Father, and at whose sight the angels are struck with awe, and the glory of whose countenance shines throughout their orders.

New birth

Once you have reached the place of tears then you should understand that the mind has left the prison of this world and set its feet on the road towards the New World.

It has begun to breathe the wonderful air which is there. It begins to shed tears.

For now the birth-pangs of the spiritual infant grow strong, since grace, the common mother of us all, makes haste to give birth mystically to the soul, the image of God, into the light of the world to come.

The image restored

This shall be for you a luminous sign of the serenity of your soul: when, on examining your-self, you find yourself full of compassion for all humanity, and your heart is afflicted with pity for them, burning as though with fire, without making distinction between one person and another.

When the image of the Father becomes visible in you by means of the continual presence of these things, then you can recognize the measure of your way of life – not from your various labours, but from the transformation which your under-standing receives.

The body is then likely to be bathed in tears, as the intellect gazes on things spiritual.

True knowledge

Do not rejoice when you grow rich in the knowledge of many things; rather, once what you know is put into practice, then rejoice that it is there with you.

The former kind of knowledge without the latter will gradually leave you, and it can even lead to pride through not being put to use.

When, however, you are diligent in the second kind of knowledge, you will certainly become illumined in the first, without needing any instruction.

The eye of knowledge is experience, and its growth comes from constant labour.

Finis

These things have I written down for my own benefit and for the benefit of anyone who happens to come across this book.

I have written in accordance with what I have understood, both from contemplation on the Scriptures, and also from those who speak the truth, and a little from experience itself.

I have written, furthermore, in order that I should benefit from the prayers of those who have benefited from these words, seeing that I have toiled over them.

Sources and index

The figures in bold in the left-hand column below refer to the pages of this book. The figures in the right-hand column refer to pages in the earlier editions. M = *The Ascetical Homilies of St Isaac the Syrian* (translated by Dana Miller); W = *Mystic Treatises of Isaac of Nineveh* (translated by A.J. Wensinck); S = *The Syriac Fathers on Prayer and the Spiritual Life* (edited by Sebastian Brock). The three passages marked SB are from hitherto unpublished material.